MW01232502

Provincetown By The Sea

Eugene Ashton Perry

Provincetown By the Sea

Second Edition

THE PERRY PICTURES COMPANY

Malden   Boston   New York

THE "CAPE COD."

RACE POINT LIGHT HOUSE.

LONG POINT LIGHT.

FISH WEIRS.

THE SAN FRANCISCO

THE PRAIRIE

PROVINCETOWN HARBOR.

FISH WEIRS.

THE SAN FRANCISCO   THE PRAIRIE

PROVINCETOWN HARBOR.

VIEW FROM THE HARBOR.

VIEW FROM THE HARBOR.

STEAMBOAT "LONGFELLOW" APPROACHING THE WHARF.

COMMERCIAL STREET.

BATHERS.

ATLANTIC HOUSE.

RAILROAD STATION AND TOWN HILL.

TOWN CRIER.

GIFFORD HOUSE.

A CATCH OF MACKEREL.

PILGRIM HOUSE.

ODD FELLOWS HALL.

CONGREGATIONAL CHURCH AND TOWN HALL.

ALONG SHORE.

MAYO COTTAGE.

HARBOR AND TOWN, FROM EAST END.

ATKINS COTTAGE.

VIEW OF BEACH, FROM EAST END.

FISH HOUSES, FISH FLAKES, AND WHARF.

DRYING CODFISH.

COTTAGES, EAST END.

SAND DUNES.

PEAKED HILL BAR LIFE-SAVING STATION.

AN OLD WRECK.

USING THE BREECHES BUOY

HIGHLAND LIGHT AND THE CLIFFS.

CPSIA information can be obtained at www.ICGtesting.com
Printed in the USA
LVOW050854240512

282958LV00006B/8/P